India

Come on a journey of discovery

Elaine Jackson

Teacher Created Resources

First published in the United States by
QEB Publishing
23062 La Cadena Drive
Laguna Hills
Irvine, CA 92653

This edition published by
Teacher Created Resources, Inc.
6421 Industry Way
Westminster, CA 92683

www.teachercreated.com

Library of Congress Control Number: 2004101782

ISBN 978 1 4206 8283 0

Written by Elaine Jackson
Designed by Starry Dog Books Ltd
Editor Christine Harvey
Maps by PCGraphics (UK) Ltd

Creative Director Louise Morley
Editorial Manager Jean Coppendale

Printed and bound in China

Picture credits
Key: t = top, b = bottom, m = middle, c = center,
l = left, r = right

Corbis Amit Bhargara 23m,/ Sheidan Collins 24,
/ David Cumming 19t,/ Bennett Dean 22,/ David H.
Wells 25t,/ Blaine Harrington III 27t,/ Chris Hellier 27b,
/ Robert Holmes 15m, 17t,/ Jeremy Horner 13,/ Earl
Kowall 18m, 18b, 24t,/ Caroline Penn 17b,/ Christian
Simonpietri 6-7; **Getty** Glen Allison title page, 2t,
14b,/ Nicholas VeVore 25b,/ Mark Downey 16-17,
/ Ben Edwards 15t,/ Ingo Jezierski 2b,/ Santokh
Kochar 2m, 7t,/ Phillip Lee Harvey 26b,/ Chris Noble
7b,/ Slede Preis 9b, 17m,/ Martin Puddy 8-9,/ Herb
Schmitz 22-23,/ David Sutherland 20-21,/ Art Wolfe
21t; **Greta Jensen** 9br, 10-11, 11tr, 23tr.

International and regional boundaries in areas of
dispute and conflict are shown as a simplification
of the true situation. This simplification has been
undertaken because this book is aimed at the
7-11 age group.

Words in **bold** can be
found in the glossary
on page 28.

Contents

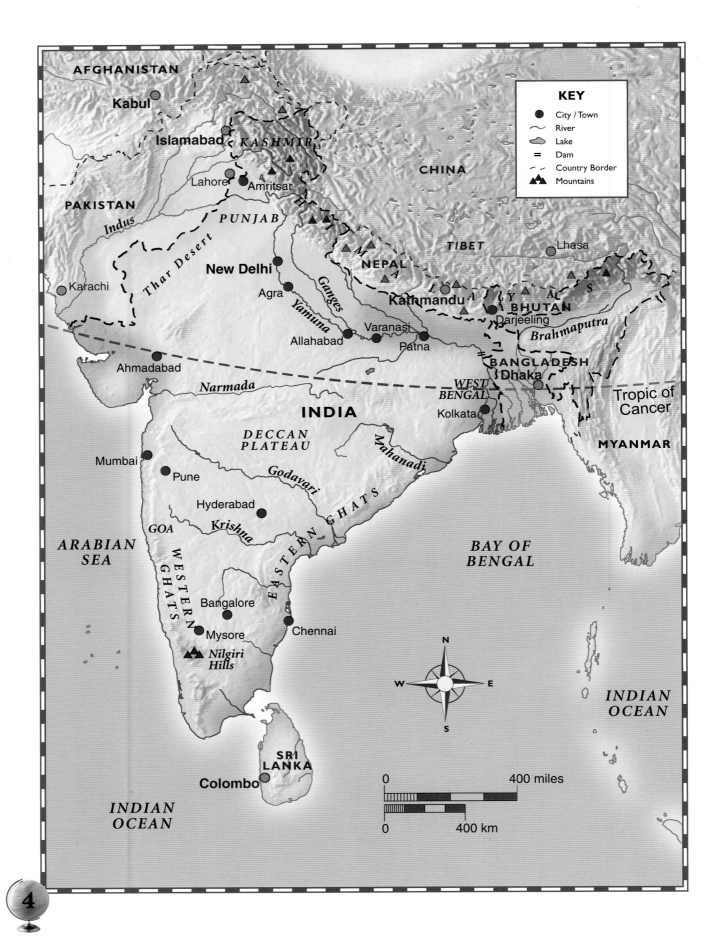

AFGHANISTAN

Kabul

Islamabad

KASHMIR

CHINA

Lahore
Amritsar

PAKISTAN

PUNJAB

Indus

Thar Desert

TIBET

Lhasa

New Delhi

NEPAL

Agra

Ganges

Kathmandu

BHUTAN

Yamuna

Darjeeling

Brahmaputra

Varanasi

Allahabad

Patna

BANGLADESH
Dhaka

Karachi

Ahmadabad

Narmada

*WEST
BENGAL*

Tropic of
Cancer

INDIA

Kolkata

MYANMAR

*DECCAN
PLATEAU*

Mahanadi

Mumbai

Pune

Godavari

Hyderabad

GOA

Krishna

*ARABIAN
SEA*

W E S T E R N   G H A T S

E A S T E R N   G H A T S

*BAY OF
BENGAL*

Bangalore

Mysore

Chennai

*INDIAN
OCEAN*

*Nilgiri
Hills*

*SRI
LANKA*

Colombo

*INDIAN
OCEAN*

KEY

● City / Town
〜 River
　 Lake
= Dam
- - - Country Border
▲▲ Mountains

N
W　E
S

0　　　　　　400 miles

0　　　　　　400 km

4

Where in the world is India?

India lies in the southern part of the **continent** of Asia. India is surrounded by the Arabian Sea to the west, the Bay of Bengal to the east, the Indian Ocean to the south, and the mountains of the Himalayas to the north (see opposite). India has borders with Bangladesh, Pakistan, and several other countries.

India has a huge population. More than a billion (1,000,000,000) people live in India. That is almost one-sixth of all the human beings on Earth, and about four times the population of the United States! This makes India the world's second most heavily populated nation after China.

▼ India and its place in the world

India

▲ The national flag of India

Did you know?

Official name Republic of India
Location Southern Asia
Neighboring countries
Bangladesh, Pakistan, Nepal, Afghanistan, Sri Lanka, China, Bhutan
Surrounding seas and oceans
Arabian Sea, Bay of Bengal, Indian Ocean
Length of coastline 3,498 miles
Capital city New Delhi
Area 1,269,346 square miles
Population 1,129,866,154 (2007 estimate)
Life expectancy Male: 57, Female: 58
Religions Hinduism (80%), Islam (14%), Christianity, Sikhism, Buddhism, Jainism
Languages Official languages: Hindi and English. There are also fifteen other different regional languages.
Climate Tropical monsoon
Highest mountain range Himalayas
Major rivers Ganges (length: 1,557 miles), Indus (length: 1,800 miles), Brahmaputra (length: 1,800 miles)
Currency Rupee

What is India like?

A land of contrasts

As you travel through India, you might think that it feels like two separate countries: **rural** India and **urban** India. Tens of millions of people live in very poor conditions in villages, where the ways of farming and growing food have not changed for hundreds of years. At the same time, sprawling Indian cities are thriving with modern, high-tech **industries** and crowded, polluted streets.

▼ In Indian cities, many small stores are often crammed together, selling everything from suits to tongue scrapers!

Traveling across the landscape

The physical landscape of India is also varied. In the north, there are the mountain ranges of the Himalayas. This area has some of the world's highest mountain peaks and the largest snow-covered areas outside the polar regions. South of the Himalayas is the huge, flat area of land through which the mighty Ganges River flows. Southern India contains an area of high, flat land called the Deccan Plateau. This has mountain ranges on each side, called the Eastern and Western Ghats.

▼ Many of India's rural areas are very poor, and farmers use slow, old-fashioned farming methods.

A mixed climate

India's climate is very mixed. As you travel around the country, you will feel cold in the mountainous areas, which have snow all year round, then hot in the dry areas of **arid** desert, where there is little or no rainfall. Most of the rain falls in one season only: in four months during the summer.

A spiritual country

Religion is very important to the Indian people. India's flag shows that people of different religions are united in one country. The orange stripe is for **Hindus**, the green for **Muslims**, the white for peace, and the **Wheel of Ashoka** for **Buddhists**.

▼ The snowcapped Himalayas are in northern India.

Climate — traveling through the seasons

The cooler months

Most of India has a **tropical** climate with three main seasons.

If you travel to India during the cooler months, between October and March, you will notice the hot, dry winds that blow across India from northeast to southwest.

The wetter months

If you travel in the summer months, from June through September, you will experience the **monsoon** winds. They blow from the southwest and sweep across the country. They reach India from the Indian Ocean and carry a lot of water with them. You will notice how unusual the monsoon winds are, because the rain that falls from them is very heavy, the drops are very large, and the rain feels hot on your skin.

▼ Everyday life continues as usual in India, even when the streets are flooded after the monsoon rains.

CLIMATE DATA FOR MUMBAI (BOMBAY)

	Jan.	Feb.	March	April	May	June	July	Aug.	Sept.	Oct	Nov.	Dec.
Temperature (°F)	75	77	80	86	84	79	79	80	82	79	79	77
Rainfall (inches)	1/16	1/16	1/16	0	1/3	18	30	14	10	3¼	1/3	1/16

INDIA'S THREE SEASONS

Months	Temperature	Rainfall
October — March	75–77°F	Dry: below ½ inch per month
April — May	82–88°F	Dry: below 1¼ inches per month
June — September	80–84°F	Very wet: over 23 inches per month

June through September

October through March

ASIA
HOT AIR
LOW PRESSURE

INDIA

Arabian
Sea

Bay of
Bengal

Equator

INDIAN OCEAN

ASIA
DENSE COLD AIR
HIGH PRESSURE

INDIA

Arabian
Sea

Bay of
Bengal

Equator

INDIAN
OCEAN

◀ The red arrows show which way the winds blow across India during the wet and cool seasons.

Learn about Geeta

❓ In July, Geeta will visit her grandparents in Mumbai (Bombay). What kind of clothes will she need to take?

❓ Geeta lives in Atlanta, Georgia. How would the rainfall in Mumbai at this time be similar to, or different from, the rainfall in Atlanta?

Traveling through the countryside

Village life

Two-thirds of the people of India live in villages. As you travel through the villages, you will see people farming small plots of land. You will notice the whole family working on the land, including children. Many children in India cannot afford to go to school, and less than half of the population of India can read and write.

Farm work

In the countryside, farming is often done by hand. Most farmers do not have enough money to buy tractors, and so use traditional farming methods dating back hundreds of years. Many villages have no running water or **sewage** facilities, so diseases are still a problem in rural areas.

Cows

Cows, **oxen**, and water buffalo are very important in Indian village life. Often, their horns are brightly painted to show that they are owned by a particular family. Cows' milk and dairy products (such as butter, cheese, and yogurt) are important food sources for village people. The cow is **sacred** in the Hindu religion, and its meat is never eaten. Cow manure is traditionally used as a fertilizer and a fuel.

▼ Families work hard on their farms. Women and girls help with weeding and harvesting the crops, in addition to milking the animals, carrying water, preparing meals, and taking care of smaller children.

▲ Most farmers in India cannot afford modern farm machinery, and use oxen and water buffalo to pull carts and plows. Any products that the family does not need are taken by cart to the market ('haat') to sell or trade for other goods.

Read this extract from Suribi's diary about life in her village.

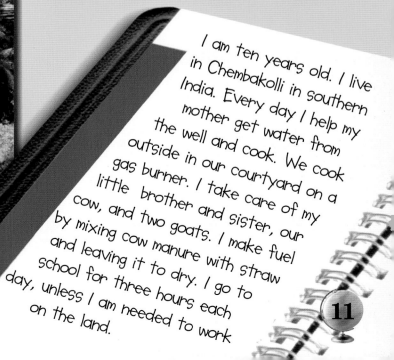

I am ten years old. I live in Chembakolli in southern India. Every day I help my mother get water from the well and cook. We cook outside in our courtyard on a little gas burner. I take care of my brother and sister, our cow, and two goats. I make fuel by mixing cow manure with straw and leaving it to dry. I go to school for three hours each day, unless I am needed to work on the land.

11

Traveling through the farming areas

The farming year is linked to the monsoon rain cycle. Farming varies from region to region, and it depends on the climate, soil, and landscape.

The northwest
Our trip through the farming areas begins in Ladakh, where cabbages, barley, and potatoes grow well. Fruit and rice are grown in Kashmir. Wheat, sugar, rice, potatoes, and legumes are grown in the rich plains of Punjab.

Around the Ganges River
The huge plains here are India's main grain-growing area, producing wheat, rice, corn, and legumes. A lot of fruit (such as lemons, apples, tomatoes), vegetables (such as cauliflower, eggplant, spinach), and spices are grown here.

◀ Lots of top-quality fruit and vegetables are sold at outdoor street markets.

The northeast
India is the world's biggest **exporter** of tea. Tea is grown on huge plantations on the northern plains of Assam and Darjeeling. It is grown where there is heavy rainfall and good drainage, and where the land is **terraced** to prevent **soil erosion**. Many workers are needed to prepare the land, weed the plantations, and pick the tea leaves from the bushes.

Central India
As you travel through central India you will see fields of cotton and food grains, such as millet. Rice and sugar cane are grown in the coastal regions of the south and east because the climate is wetter there. Basmati rice is grown in the foothills of the Himalayas. Rice production is very labor-intensive, and most of the work is done by hand.

The south
You will see coconut palm trees all over southern India. Spices, coffee, bananas, and cashews are also grown here for export.

▼ Tea leaves are placed in a basket strapped to the worker's back.

Did you know?

Most of the rice grown every year in India is eaten within the country, except basmati rice, which is exported.

Amazing, but true!

In 2001, India produced 22.5 percent of the world's rice and was the second biggest producer after China.

▼ This map shows the main areas where food products are grown.

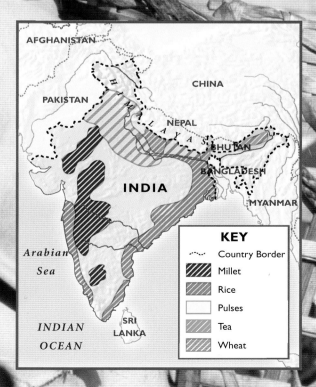

AFGHANISTAN

PAKISTAN

CHINA

HIMALAYAS

NEPAL

BHUTAN

BANGLADESH

INDIA

MYANMAR

Arabian Sea

SRI LANKA

INDIAN OCEAN

KEY

- ┄┄┄ Country Border
- Millet
- Rice
- Pulses
- Tea
- Wheat

13

A city tour of India

Mumbai (Bombay)

Mumbai (Bombay) is India's largest city and port. It is also India's leading **industrial** city. Cotton textiles, cars, chemicals, and machinery are all manufactured there. If you visit Mumbai, you will see huge houses and great wealth, but also poor **slums** full of shacks and street children.

Mumbai is also the center of India's movie industry, known as "Bollywood," and it produces more movies than anywhere else in the world—even Hollywood!

New Delhi

New Delhi is the capital city of India. It is an important business center, with many banks and offices. There are also factories manufacturing electronics, electrical appliances, chemicals, textiles, and automobile parts.

Kolkata

Kolkata is India's second largest city. It is an industrial center and major port. As in other Indian cities, wealth exists beside deep poverty, unemployment, and overcrowding.

▲ Posters for "Bollywood" movies are usually colorful and dramatic, just like the films.

A Mumbai child

Deepi is twelve years old and lives with her parents and brother in a large house in Mumbai. Deepi's father is a scientist. He works in the chemical industry, making medicines. Her mother is a teacher. Deepi and her brother attend school every day and Deepi wants to be a doctor when she grows up.

▶ Kolkata's slums are home to many street children.

A Kolkata child
Eight-year-old Manni is an orphan and lives on the streets. Every day, he looks through garbage and begs on the streets for money to pay for food and shelter. Sometimes rich tourists give him a few rupees.

Bangalore
Located in south-central India, Bangalore is regarded as the most modern of India's cities. It has parks, wide streets, big supermarkets, and Internet cafés everywhere. Bangalore is India's high-tech center, famous for computer companies, aircraft industries, and international **telecommunication** services.

▲ New Delhi is full of people, traffic, and cows, which wander wherever they want.

15

Why tourists travel to India

Things to see and do
India is a fascinating country. It has become a place many people travel to for adventure. Tourists from all over the world visit India each year.

The Golden Triangle
Many visitors to India begin with "The Golden Triangle." The starting point is Delhi, and then they go to Agra to see the famous Taj Mahal. The next stop is Jaipur. It is known as the "Pink City," because its old buildings are a yellow-pink color.

The Ganges River
Other visitors go to India to make a **pilgrimage** to the holy Ganges River. They take part in religious ceremonies and celebrations.

Beach vacations
For many travelers to India, Goa is the place to visit. Goa is very popular with tourists who want to sunbathe on sandy beaches and swim in the warm water of the Arabian Sea.

▼ Around 20,000 workers built the Taj Mahal.

◀ Goa's beaches are fringed with palm trees. Early and late in the day, you will *see* fishermen on the beach hauling in their catch using sturdy ropes. They are very happy if you lend a hand!

Some take the opportunity to try water sports, such as windsurfing and sailing. Others visit tiny fishing villages and wander around the colorful markets. At the markets, you can buy beautiful silks, carved figurines, silver and brass objects, finely crafted jewelry, and carpets. Haggling (bargaining) with the market sellers is part of the fun for tourists, and you can find many fantastic bargains.

Amazing, but true!

The Taj Mahal at Agra took twenty-three years to build. It was built by Emperor Shah Jahan in memory of his second wife, Mumtaz Mahal. She died in 1630 while having a baby. It is said that the emperor was so heartbroken that his hair turned gray overnight.

▼ Shawls, blankets, and highly patterned fabrics are all found in local markets.

Getting around India

On the move

India is very large, and you will probably use different forms of transportation to travel around. India is crisscrossed by the largest railway system in Asia.

▼ Most people in India do not own a car, so public transportation is always in demand.

Rickshaws

The **rickshaw** is the world's oldest form of wheeled transportation. Millions of rickshaws are still in use in India today. They are used by businessmen going to work, children going to and from school, people going shopping, as well as tourists, who enjoy the novelty of this cheap method of travel.

◄ Only in Kolkata are rickshaws still pulled by people. In other cities, bicycles are used to pull them.

▼ Local buses are often dangerously overcrowded.

▼ Local buses are often dangerously overcrowded.

India's busy roads

In the overcrowded cities and towns of India, you will be amazed at how busy the main streets are. They are crammed with cars, buses, trucks, rickshaws, ox carts, bicycles, and pedestrians, all competing for the limited space on the streets. High traffic levels have increased pollution in the cities. This is a serious environmental concern for the country.

In India's villages, where the conditions of roads are poor and a car ride can be very bumpy, the locals often use ox carts to travel around. The ride is slow but safe.

Read Geeta's diary entry about her first trip in a rickshaw.

Inside the rickshaw it was very hot, and our ride was slow, bumpy, and noisy. The street was so busy with people, bicycles, other rickshaws, motorcycles, ox carts, overloaded trucks, cars, overcrowded buses (with people hanging from the sides and roofs!), beggars, and thin, humpbacked cows.

19

The Ganges River

India's great life source

If you travel along the length of the Ganges River, you will travel about 1,550 miles across India into Bangladesh, where the river enters the Bay of Bengal. The river is the life source of the country. More than 350 million people use the waters of the Ganges River in their daily lives. The water is used in their homes for drinking, for cleaning and washing, in their factories, on their farms, and as a means of transportation.

The holy river

This river lies at the heart of India's religious beliefs. Hindus consider the river to be the goddess Ganga, and so its water is holy to them. All along the river there are **ghats**, where **pilgrims** can enter the river to bathe. People **cremate** (burn) their dead on its banks and throw the remains into the river, in the belief that the goddess Ganga will take the dead to heaven.

▼ The holiest of India's cities is Varanasi, where thousands of pilgrims wash in the river while praying. Even in the winter, they brave the freezing temperatures.

▲ Saddhus are Hindu holy men who give up ordinary life and devote themselves to religious practice.

Read this extract from Anil's autobiography.

I was eleven years old when I first went to bathe in the Ganges River with my father. Early one morning, we walked with thousands of other Hindus down to the bathing ghat. There we prayed, lit **diva lamps**, and floated them down the river. Seeing the huge number of glowing diva lamps floating in the early morning mist is a sight I will never forget.

Traveling along the Ganges River

▶ The bare patches used to be covered in forests.

The journey begins

If you decide to travel the length of the River Ganges, your trip will begin at the **source** of the river at the Gangotri **glacier**, in the foothills of the Himalayas. As the Ganges runs through northern India, you will see how much this area has been affected by trees being cut down from the forests.

The Upper Ganges Canal

The **canal** takes water from the Ganges to **irrigate** farmland. This means that a second crop can be grown each year after the first crop has been watered by the rains of the **monsoon**.

Kanpur

Your next stop along the Ganges will be the industrial city of Kanpur. Here the leather and textile factories dump harmful wastes such as bleach, dye, and chemicals into the river. This industrial pollution, added to the human **sewage** and the remains of bodies **cremated** on the riverbanks, makes the waters of the Ganges a serious health risk.

▼ River water is used to irrigate the rice paddies (fields) so that more crops can be grown.

The Silk City

The river flows on to Bhagalpur, the "Silk City." Silk is produced from the cocoons of the silkworm caterpillars. Much of the spinning is still done by hand.

The end of the journey

Just before the Ganges leaves India and forms its **delta** in Bangladesh, you will see the Farakka **Barrage** that was built to improve navigation to the port of Kolkata (Calcutta).

◄ Heavy pollution is a major health hazard.

Read this extract from a tourist's travel journal.

Impressions of northern India

The trees had been cut down. Local people took some of the wood to use as fuel and building materials, but an international logging company that wanted to sell the lumber had cut down most of the trees. During the last monsoon season, a lot of the soil had been washed away because the trees could no longer protect the earth from the rains. There were no sounds of birds or animals.

Food — cooking and eating in India

▶ A street seller squeezes out coils of deliciously sweet jelebi mixture into bubbling oil.

My name is Srinvas. I live in southern India. We eat idlis (steamed rice cakes) and doshe (rice flour pancakes). I love bhujia and sambar (very hot vegetable stews) made with kerri (spicy sauce).

My name is Raju. I am a Sikh and I live in Punjab. I like to eat parathas (bread), lamb curry, and potatoes cooked in spices.

My name is Suribi. I live in Goa. I like to eat Bombay duck. Bombay duck is not a duck! It is fish that is curried or fried.

My name is Nitan and I live in Kashmir. My favorite foods include rogan josh (curried lamb), koftas (spicy meatballs), and yakhni (stew with fennel seeds and curry spices).

Indian food

Indian dishes are colorful and use many spices. As you travel around India, you will eat different meals, depending on two things: the ingredients grown in a particular region and the religion followed there. Many Indians are vegetarians. Hindus do not eat beef. Muslims do not eat pork.

How to eat

Even though knives and forks are used in India, eating with the fingers of your right hand shows good manners. You are able to feel and appreciate the texture of the food.

Desserts and drinks

Indian children love sweet foods and drinks. *Halva*, *ladoos*, and *burfi* are delicious sweets made from milk products. Favorite drinks include *lassi* (a cold buttermilk drink), coconut milk, and *chai* (tea). In large cities and towns, children also drink carbonated soda.

▲ Press the food firmly together between your fingers, then scoop it up to your mouth to eat.

▼ Market spices are sold by weight.

25

Visiting sacred places in India

Geeta's teacher asked her to find out about Indian religions and special holy places while she was visiting her grandparents in Mumbai. Read the extracts from her travel journal.

Islam
Interesting facts
* Followers of Islam are called **Muslims**.
* The Qur'an is the holy book of Islam.
* Muslims believe the Qur'an contains the exact words Allah (God) said to **Mohammed**, his prophet on Earth.
* Muslims worship in places called **mosques**.
* During prayers, parts of the Qur'an are read five times a day.

PLACE TO VISIT
Kashmir is an important Islamic region.

Buddhism
Interesting facts
* Many followers of Buddhism live in remote areas of the Himalayas.
* Some **Buddhists** originally came from Tibet, which is north of India.
* Buddhists believe in a peaceful existence and do not cause harm to any living things.
* Buddhists paint prayers on cloths, which are known as prayer flags. These are hung from cords and stretched out like clotheslines across the sky, because Buddhists hope the prayers will travel with the wind.

PLACE TO VISIT
The monastery at Leh, in Ladakh, which is in the far north of India.

▼ The Buddhist monastery at Leh, in Ladakh.

▶ The Golden Temple is built on a beautiful pool. Visitors must take off their shoes.

▶ Hindus offer sticks of incense, sweet treats, and flowers to their gods.

Sikhism
Interesting facts
* Sikhism includes elements from both Hinduism and Islam.
* The holy book is called Guru Granth Sahib. It is kept at the Golden Temple.
* Sikh men must never cut the hair on their face or head. They wear their hair coiled under a turban.

PLACE TO VISIT
Golden Temple (Gurdawa), in Amritsar, Punjab.

Hinduism
Interesting facts
* Eighty percent of the Indian people follow the Hindu religion.
* **Hindus** believe that Hindu gods and goddesses represent the different qualities and powers of the one supreme God.
* Hindus believe that the gods and goddesses live in **temples** and **shrines**.
* Hindus have many festivals and celebrations, for example Diwali and Holi.
* Hindus believe that the place where any rivers meet is sacred. Stepped platforms, called **ghats**, are built to enable **pilgrims** to bathe more easily in the Ganges River.

PLACE TO VISIT
Allahabad, where the Ganges, the Yamuna, and the mythical Saraswati River meet, is the holiest place on Earth for Hindus to bathe.

▶ A Hindu girl makes an offering to the gods.

Glossary

arid
a place having little or no rain

barrage
a structure or bridge in a river that directs water in a particular direction

Buddhists
followers of a religion of India and Asia

canal
a manmade river

cremate
to burn a dead body

delta
a flat area at the mouth of a river

diva lamps
small, bowl-shaped container, sometimes clay, with oil inside and a single wick that is set alight

exporter
a person or company that sells goods to other countries

ghats
special steps for bathing in rivers

glacier
a slow-moving mass of ice and snow

Hindus
followers of one of the main religions of India

industries
groups of companies that make a particular product, such as steel

irrigation
bringing water to land for farming

Mohammed
the Prophet of Islam

monsoon
the annual wet season

mosques
places where Muslims gather and pray

Muslims
followers of the religion of Islam

ox (*plural form:* oxen)
an animal like a cow that is used on farms

pilgrimage
a journey made for spiritual purposes

pilgrims
people on a pilgrimage

rickshaw
a small vehicle pulled by a person, or a bicycle

rural
in the countryside

sacred
viewed as special or holy by a religion

sewage
liquid waste from toilets

shrines
small temples that honor a particular god or holy person

Sikhs
followers of Sikhism, a religion of India

slums
very poor areas of a city

soil erosion
when soil is washed away

source
the place where a river starts

telecommunications
telephone, radio, and television networks

temples
places where Hindus and Buddhists pray

terraced
a hillside cut into a series of flat levels

tropical
relating to weather; very hot, humid climate

urban
in the city

Wheel of Ashoka
a symbol of India, named after an Indian emperor

Index

Teaching ideas and activities for children

The **Travel Through** series offers up-to-date information and cross-curricular knowledge in subject areas such as geography, language arts, mathematics, history, and social studies. The series enables children to develop an overview ("the big picture") of each country. This overview reflects the huge diversity and richness of the life and culture of each country. The series aims to prevent the development of misconceptions, stereotypes, and prejudices, which often develop when the focus of a study narrows too quickly onto a small locality within a country. The books will help children gain access to this overview, and also develop an understanding of the interconnectedness of places. They contribute to children's geographical knowledge, skills, and understanding, and help them to make sense of the world around them.

The following activities promote thinking skills and creativity. The activities in section A are designed to help children develop critical thinking skills, while the activities in section B are designed to promote different types of learning styles.

A: ACTIVITIES TO DEVELOP THINKING SKILLS
ACTIVITIES TO PROMOTE RESEARCH AND RECALL OF FACTS
Ask the child to:
• make an alphabet book for a young child, illustrating the contrasts in India.
• research and investigate a mountain environment (such as the Himalayas). The child could present the information in a poster or computer presentation.

ACTIVITIES TO USE INFORMATION TO SOLVE PROBLEMS

Ask the child to:

• find out, by using reference books or the Internet, how to make some Indian food or a diva lamp and write instructions for how to do this.

• make notes to explain the reasons why the streets in Indian cities are so polluted and crowded.

ACTIVITIES TO PROMOTE UNDERSTANDING

Ask the child to:

• replicate a simple map or picture of India. If you are working with a group of children, place the children in small groups of equal sizes. Tell them they are going to reproduce the map or picture you have. In their groups, ask them to number themselves and to discuss strategies they could use to reproduce your picture. Call each number, one at a time, to look at the picture for two minutes. Then ask them to go back and draw what they can remember, while discussing the picture and strategies with their group. Give the children five minutes to do this. Then call the next member of the group, and so on. At the end, show the children the original and ask them to evaluate each group's work.

ACTIVITIES TO ENCOURAGE ANALYTICAL THINKING

Ask the child to:

• compare and contrast life in a village in India with life in an Indian city.

• write a report about recreational pursuits or sports in India.

ACTIVITIES TO STIMULATE CREATIVITY

Ask the child to:

• make a collage or painting of the Himalayas and/or a rice-growing area.

• design a word search, including geographical words, on a specific subject, such as the Himalayas.

ACTIVITIES TO HELP CHILDREN USE EVIDENCE TO FORM OPINIONS AND EVALUATE CONSEQUENCES OF DECISIONS

Ask the child to:

• write a report about who in India would appreciate the monsoon rains and who would not.

• list the consequences of what would happen if the monsoon winds failed to bring rain.

B: ACTIVITIES BASED ON DIFFERENT LEARNING STYLES

ACTIVITIES FOR LINGUISTIC LEARNERS

Ask the child to:

- write a rap to promote India as a good place to go on vacation.
- write a newspaper report about traffic jams in Kolkata or Mumbai.

ACTIVITIES FOR MATHEMATICAL LEARNERS

Ask the child to:

- find out about the population of India, or a city in India, over the past ten years, collate this information, and represent it in a graph.

ACTIVITIES FOR VISUAL LEARNERS

Ask the child to:

- locate the major cities and rivers on a map of India.
- design a poster or comic strip to show what life in Mumbai is like.

ACTIVITIES FOR KINESTHETIC LEARNERS

Ask the child to:

- make a model of the Ganges River from its source to the mouth.
- create a dance to represent the coming of the monsoon, the increasing flow of water in the rivers, and the growth of new vegetation.

ACTIVITIES FOR MUSICAL LEARNERS

Ask the child to:

- listen to some Indian music and identify the instruments used.
- create and perform a simple tune that is representational of Indian rhythms.

ACTIVITIES FOR INTERPERSONAL LEARNERS

Ask the child to:

- plan a welcome for an Indian visitor who is unable to communicate in English.

ACTIVITIES FOR INTRAPERSONAL LEARNERS

Ask the child to:

- express how he or she would feel riding along an Indian street in a rickshaw.

ACTIVITIES FOR NATURALISTIC LEARNERS

Ask the child to:

- make notes about the pros and cons of logging in the foothills of the Himalayas. Get him or her to prepare a speech for a debate, either for or against.